CHOY LAY FUT KUNG-FU

CHOY LAY FUT KUNG-FU
CHINESE ART OF SELF-DEFENSE

by Leo T. Fong

OHARA 🅿 PUBLICATIONS, INCORPORATED

BURBANK, CALIFORNIA

Acknowledgements

The completion of any great project is seldom a solo performance. The publishing of CHOY LAY FUT KUNG-FU is no exception. My sincere appreciation to Mr. Ed Ikuta for the excellent photography, and to Mr. Richard Clark and Mr. Richard Garvey who endured many hours under hot lights to pose for the pictures with me.

©Ohara Publications, Incorporated 1972
All rights reserved
Printed in the United States of America
Library of Congress Catalog Card Number: 70-181999

Thirteenth Printing 1983

ISBN 0-89750-035-0

PREFACE

During the past decade many techniques and training systems of individual combat have been introduced through books and through individual and group instruction. No single martial art has experienced greater popularity than Karate. Many have speculated upon the reasons for this rapid growth. Having lived through the infancy stage of Karate in the United States, it is my opinion that the American public responded to Karate because there were instructors willing to teach the art to those who were willing to learn, regardless of color or creed. In Karate the American public saw not only a system of self-defense but an excellent form of exercise and sport in which men, women and children could participate without the possibility of serious injuries.

During Karate's early years, there were few open tournaments in the U.S. Those who did participate in tournaments revealed their systems and styles by their techniques. The Korean stylist fought like a Korean stylist, the Japanese stylist fought like a Japanese stylist and the Kenpo stylist fought like a Kenpo stylist. However, as the number of tournaments increased and competition became keener, it became difficult to identify a competitor's system by the techniques used. The evolution of an American style of Karate became evident as competitors borrowed from other systems. Stylistic purity gave way to practicality as participants searched for techniques that would score consistently. This evolution toward a more practical style of fighting came about through the contributions of players from many styles and systems who were willing to risk their secrets by participating in open tournaments and demonstrations.

Very few ideas are original. It is through the inspiration of others that our creativity is activated. The purpose of CHOY LAY FUT KUNG-FU is not to introduce another "superior" system of individual combat, but to share this one style of training with the martial arts world in the hope that something within this volume might contribute to that world.

This book will by no means make you an expert in six months. For the beginner it can serve as a starting point. For the advanced student it attempts to provide practical and meaningful direction. Like life, the martial arts should involve a process of growth and discovery. Sometimes a life, an idea, even a word, can reveal to us a new truth that changes us for the better. If CHOY LAY FUT can accomplish this for you, it will have been a worthwhile endeavor.

Leo T. Fong

DEDICATION

To my wife Libertad, whose continued encouragement has been a source of power, and to Mr. Bruce Lee, a colleague and friend, whose keen insights have been a great help in seeing the martial arts in their totality.

ABOUT THE AUTHOR

LEO TIM FONG was born in Canton, China in 1929 but immigrated to the United States with his parents when he was only five years old. He graduated from Hendrix College in Conway, Arkansas with a B.A. degree in physical education, and from Southern Methodist University in Dallas, Texas with a B.D. degree in theology. More recently, he has earned a master's degree in social work with a major in psychotherapy.

Having participated in track, tennis, football and boxing since his high school days, Mr. Fong has always found sports to be a way of life. In fact, his training with gloves at Hendrix College proved to be much more than an energy-charged outlet from studies, and he was proclaimed the 1949-51 collegiate boxing champion and a 1950-52 Arkansas AAU finalist. In 1953, while at SMU, he fought his way to the Southwestern Golden Gloves finals.

With the completion of his theology degree in 1954, Mr. Fong was given a pastoral assignment in Sacramento, California, the first step in a career dedicated to reaching and helping people. As a minister, he worked to dissolve the boundaries between the pulpit and parishioners, particularly those lines seemingly separating the Church from its children. What good was theory if it didn't relate to actual experience? In Sacramento, and at subsequent assignments in Vallejo, Stockton and Modesto, California, he worked to

find a viable means of communicating with young people in a way which they could understand and accept.

Over the years, Mr. Fong found that the martial arts gave him the opportunity to reach people in a way the Church could not. His extensive training in Judo, Ju-Jitsu, Tae Kwan Do and Kung-Fu gave him a tangible means of expressing what words could not portray.

Today the author is not preaching but, rather, sharing his 12 years of practical experience in Choy Lay Fut and Sil Lum Kung-Fu with students of all ages. And they listen.

CONTENTS

A BRIEF HISTORY OF CHOY LAY FUT 11

FUNDAMENTALS OF CHOY LAY FUT 13

HORSE STANCES OF CHOY LAY FUT 14

CHOY LAY FUT HORSE FORM 19

CHOY LAY FUT EXERCISES 37

ELEMENTAL AID TO CHEUNG KUNE 43

CHEUNG KUNE: The Long Range Fist
of Choy Lay Fut 67

APPLICATIONS OF CHOY LAY FUT 143

DEFENSE AND COUNTER TECHNIQUES 144

ATTACK TECHNIQUES 173

A BRIEF HISTORY OF CHOY LAY FUT KUNG-FU

The exact origins of Kung-Fu are not known. Down through the centuries many nations have claimed techniques as their own and have offered colorful, if sometimes contradictory, legends to prove their claims. To give a complete and accurate history of Kung-Fu is impossible. Too many of the records have been lost and destroyed over the centuries. However, Kung-Fu historians generally agree that the art emigrated from India to China around the year 525 A.D.

Legend has it that Daruma Taishi traveled hundreds of miles through the rugged Himalaya Mountains to China in order to instruct the Liang Dynasty in the tenets of Buddhism. Upon his arrival in China, Daruma purportedly imposed such a demanding pace and rigid discipline on his student monks that they collapsed one by one from sheer physical and mental exhaustion. In subsequent sessions Daruma supposedly pointed out to the students that although Buddhism places great emphasis on the spirit and salvation of the soul, the body and soul are inseparable. The physical condition affects the status of the spirit. In their weakened condition, the monks could never perform the ascetic discipline required to reach a state of true enlightenment.

According to legend, Daruma began to teach members of the Sil Lum Monastery a form of physical and mental exercise called *eki-kinkyo* to strengthen the body and mind, not only for self-defense against armed marauders, but also as a vehicle to reach greater spiritual heights.

From the Sil Lum Monastery the monks migrated across Asia, teaching the tenets of Buddhism and Kung-Fu. As the years passed, original Sil Lum forms and techniques were revised and modified until many branches and systems of Kung-Fu had come into being.

One of the most popular systems to emerge during these years was Choy Lay Fut, which was developed by Chan Heung, a native of Gung Mui Village in Kwang Tung Province. As was often the case with Southern Chinese youths, Chan Heung was introduced to the popular southern Sil Lum style of Hung Kuen by his uncle. Later, he trained with an instructor by the name of Lay Yau Saan. Yearning for still more knowledge, Chan Heung went to Mount Law Fow, where he sought out a Buddhist monk by the name of Choy Fook. Eventually, Chan Heung combined all his learning to form his own style, the Choy Lay Fut system, named in honor of his previous instructors Choy Fook and Lay Yau Saan. Because Hung Kuen is one of the many branches of the Sil Lum Buddhist Temple, the term Fut was included.

One of the most famous practitioners of Choy Lay Fut was Chang Hung Sing, the leading disciple of founder Chan Heung, and a very popular Chinese boxing instructor in Fut Saan, Southern China. In his honor Choy Lay Fut training halls are now usually referred to as Hung Sing *kwoon* (training halls).

Essentially, Choy Lay Fut is a long-range style of boxing that relies heavily on a strong horse stance. It is best known for its joint locking techniques, its backfist, its downward scraping swing and its knuckle fist. In addition, there are many empty hand sets *(kata)* in this southern style: the Long Range Fist, the Buddhist Fist, T'ai, Ping, Teen, Gok Fists and others. Weapons sets include the Baat Gwa Lance, Willow Leaf Double Swords and the Eighteen Staff.

Fundamentals of Choy Lay Fut

Footwork is an integral part of all fighting arts but is extremely important in Kung-Fu, especially in the Choy Lay Fut style. The originator of Choy Lay Fut believed that a strong foundation is essential to becoming a proficient Kung-Fu technician. Besides footwork, emphasis is also on the horse stance which is, in theory, compared to a young tree that grows into maturity. The roots of the young tree are shallow, but as it grows into maturity, the roots deepen and the tree becomes stronger. Eventually, it is able to withstand the force of the strongest gale.

The following chapter on horse stances has been devised to build a strong foundation for Choy Lay Fut techniques. Students in Choy Lay Fut *kwoon* (schools) are not permitted to train in hand techniques until they have mastered the horse form.

It is very important to remember not to hurry through the form in horse training. Stay in one position for at least the count of ten before changing positions. As you progress, remain in each position longer. (The author has taken up to two hours to complete the form in some of his workouts.) The purpose of this type of training is to develop endurance and strength.

Horse Stances of Choy Lay Fut

Choy Lay Fut Kung-Fu is built around four basic horse stances which you must be familiar with to understand the horse form and execute the hand set (*cheung kune*) correctly. Carefully observing the details of each stance will assure you correct execution of the forms in the succeeding chapters. Practice each stance many times before proceeding to the horse form in the following chapter. However, always remember that each movement of a technique is interrelated with all the others.

In modern day Karate tournaments a variety of stances is adapted by the contestants. Many of the Kenpo stylists fight from a horse stance, similar to the ma bo stance in the Choy Lay Fut system. Tae Kwon Do practitioners often prefer the back, or ding bo, stance, and a number of the Japanese stylists fight from a stance which is similar to the gung bo. In Choy Lay Fut, no matter what stance you prefer to use, it is important to move from one to another without breaking the continuity of the techniques. If you were to begin from the *ma bo* (horse) stance, for instance, you would shift into the *gung bo* (front) stance to deliver a reverse punch. Shifting from a horse stance to a front stance with the snapping of the hips would generate more power in the delivery of that particular punch. Should your opponent block that reverse punch and attempt a counter, the shifting into a *ding bo* (cat) stance would be an effective defensive move. From that position you could counterattack with a straight lunge punch, ending in a ma bo stance. These are only a few examples of how the Choy Lay Fut stances are interrelated in a free-fighting situation. The practice of these stances, as well as hand techniques, should include a mental picture of the total situation, and its interrelatedness.

MA BO STANCE
(Regular Horse Stance)

With your body weight evenly distributed on both legs, bend your knees slightly. Point your toes inward. Place your hands on your hips, elbows parallel to the shoulders. Your upper body should be erect, your eyes looking straight ahead.

GUNG BO STANCE

With most of your weight on the front leg, stand with that leg slightly bent. Keep the back leg straight, and point your toes inward. Your front foot should be at a 90-degree angle to the side. Place your hands on your hips, elbows parallel to the shoulders. Your upper body should be erect, your eyes looking straight ahead.

DING BO STANCE

With most of your weight placed on the back leg, your front foot should only touch the floor lightly. Place your hands on your hips, elbows parallel to your shoulders. Your upper body should be erect, your eyes looking straight ahead.

Note: The ding bo stance is similar to the cat stance in Karate or the back stance in Tae Kwon Do. An excellent way to practice the ding bo stance is to shift from right to left in a straight line, remaining in position for a few minutes before shifting. Shifting backward is good practice for retreating in free-fighting.

LAU MA STANCE

With your knees slightly bent, place your left leg forward with your toes pointing about 45 degrees to your right. The right foot, with the heel slightly raised, should be aligned with your left, the knee locked against the back of the front knee. Place your hands on your hips, elbows parallel to the shoulders. Your upper body should be erect, your head facing toward the left with eyes looking straight ahead.

Note: An excellent way to practice the lau ma stance is to start out with the ma bo stance, then shift into the lau ma by twisting the front foot and dropping down into position. Remain in that stance for a few minutes and then shift into a ma bo stance. Repeat the movements over again until they can be executed without much thought.

Choy Lay Fut Horse Form

The basic direction of the Choy Lay Fut horse form is from right to left, moving in a straight line. The next series of movements begin with the closed horse stance, leading off with the right leg followed by the left into a ma bo stance. The completion of the initial four series of movements should cover a distance of 20 to 25 feet back and forth.

Although many of the movements are repetitious of the first series, and the entire form utilizes only the four basic Choy Lay Fut stances, special emphasis should be given to the following details: (1) All movements should be executed smoothly and with continuity. They should not be rigid, but firm and soft. (2) Remain in each position a few seconds before shifting to another position. (3) Keep your hands on your hips throughout the entire form, paying particular attention to your elbows, which should be parallel to the body. (4) Always keep your body erect and your head facing straight ahead. (5) When shifting from the ma bo stance to the gung bo stance, twist your hips in a snapping motion and keep the back leg tense. (6) Strive for endurance by remaining in each position from 30 seconds to two minutes. (7) When shifting positions, do not raise or lower your body, but always keep your legs slightly bent (in a half-squat position). Note: The emphasis on inhaling and exhaling is important.

The mastery of any fighting technique requires thorough practice of the basic movements. Choy Lay Fut is no exception. The horse form is lengthy, but very basic to developing strength and endurance. The perfection of this form is recommended before attempting the hand form (*cheung kune*) in the following chapter.

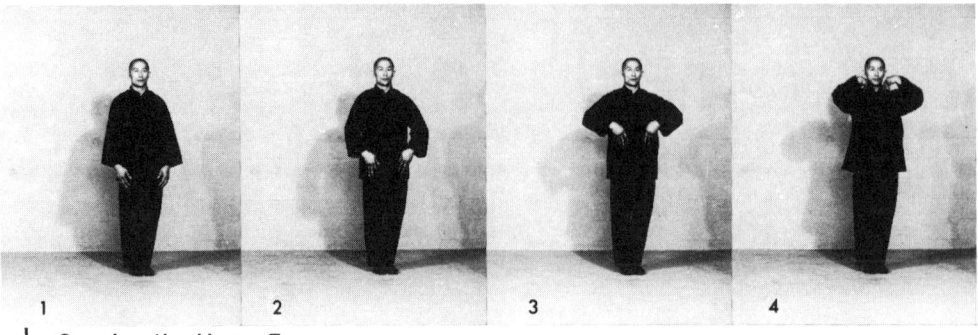

Opening the Horse Form

(1) Stand at attention with your feet together and your arms at your sides. (2) With palms close to your body, (3) inhale as you slowly raise your hands (4) to your ears. The emphasis on inhaling and exhaling is important.

Opening the Horse Form (continued)

(9) Slowly lift your hands, (10) palms facing the ceiling. (11) Inhale as you raise them to your ears, (12) turning your palms until they face the floor.

Opening the Horse Form (continued)

(17) With your hands stretched outward, inhale as you (18) begin to move your arms inward, (19) slowly rotating your palms until (20) they face each other. Note: The movement should not be rigid, but should be firm and soft.

(5) Slowly rotate your palms clockwise around your ears as you breathe out, until (6) your palms face the ceiling. (7) Slowly retract your hands (8) to your sides. All movements should be executed smoothly and with continuity.

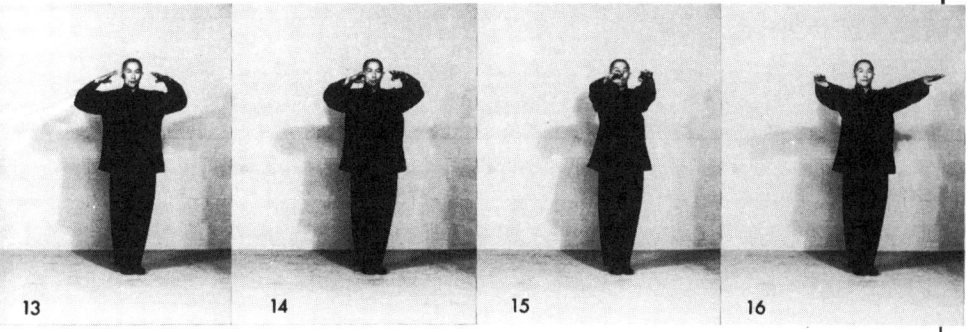

(13) Exhale as you (14) softly but firmly (15) thrust both arms forward, palms facing the floor. (16) Inhale as you begin to stretch your hands outward. Your eyes should look straight ahead at all times.

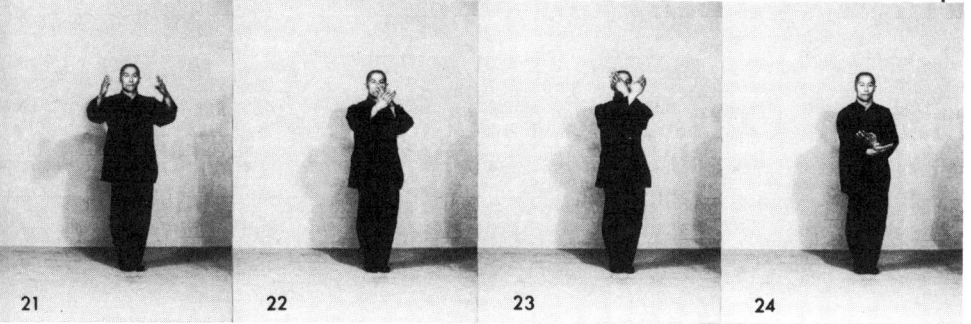

(21) Moving your palms toward each other, (22) cross your right hand over your left, (23) simultaneously bending your knees slightly. (24) Lower your hands to waist level as you exhale.

Opening the Horse Form (continued)

(25) With your knees still slightly bent and your arms at your sides, (26) raise your hands, palms down, until they are parallel to the floor. (27) Bend your elbows, (28) bringing your hands to the chest.

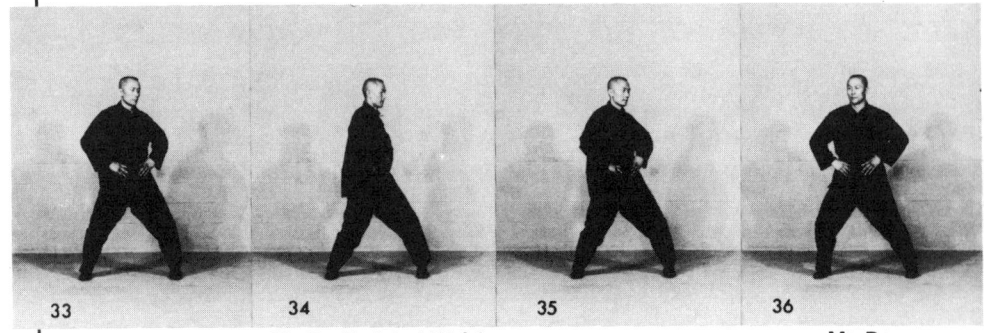

Ma Bo Twisted Waist   **Ma Bo**

To change direction, (33) twist the upper part of your body to the left, (34) without replanting your feet. (35) Your hands should remain on your hips as you (36) return to your original ma bo position.

Closed Horse   **Ma Bo**

From the ma bo stance, (41) move into a closed horse stance, (42) placing your right foot close to the left without moving your body. Repeat movements 30—42 three times before proceeding to a ma bo stance (43 & 44).

Ma Bo

(29 & 30) With your hands resting on your hips, (31) extend your right leg and (32) slide your left into a *ma bo* (horse) stance. You can repeat this exercise, moving in a straight line, to develop mobility.

Gung Bo   Ma Bo

(37) Now twist your body to the right into a *gung bo* (front stance) position by (38) shifting your weight to the right. (39) Your toes should be pointed inward. (40) Return to a ma bo position by facing the front again.

Ma Bo Twisted Waist

(45) Twist your upper body to the left, (46) without replanting your feet. (47) With your hands still on your hips, twist in the opposite direction. (48) Rotate to the right from a ma bo into a gung bo stance.

| 49 | 50 | 51 | 52 |

Gung Bo   **Left Gung Bo**

From a right gung bo position, (49) begin to twist your upper body (50) to the left into a (51) left gung bo position. (52) Your head should follow the movement, but your feet should be planted in one position.

| 57 | 58 | 59 | 60 |

Ma Bo

(57) Shift into a ma bo stance by extending your left leg as far as possible, and then your right. (58) Twist your upper body to the right, (59) keeping your lower body stationary and (60) your elbows parallel to your body.

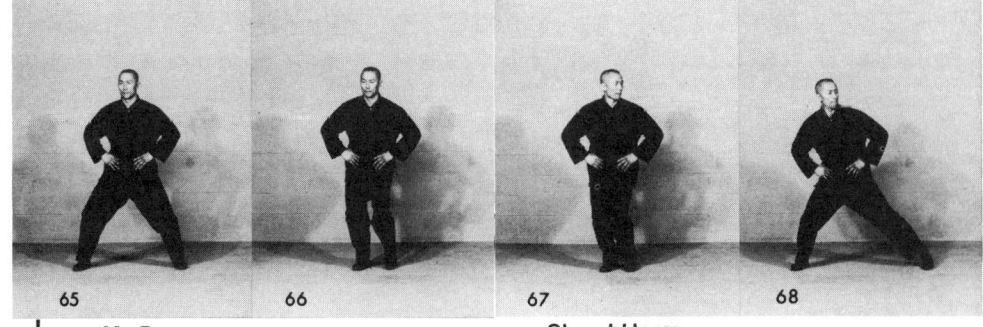

| 65 | 66 | 67 | 68 |

Ma Bo   **Closed Horse**

(65) Shift back into a ma bo stance and then into a (66) closed horse stance, (67) turning your head toward the left. Repeat movements 56-67 three times before leading off with the left leg into a ma bo position (68).

Ma Bo   Closed Horse

(53) From the left gung bo position, (54) move into a ma bo stance by facing toward the front. (55) Shift into a closed horse stance, and (56) turn your head toward the left.

Gung Bo

(61) Turn your body to the left as you begin to shift into a (62) gung bo position. (63) Your left leg is bent slightly more than (64) your right. Your eyes should follow the movement.

Ma Bo

(69) From a ma bo stance, (70) twist your upper body to the right. (71) Your lower body should remain as stationary as possible with (72) your elbows parallel to your shoulders.

Left Gung Bo

(73) From a twisted upper body position, (74) rotate to the left into a gung bo position, (75) with your left leg slightly bent and (76) your right leg extended as straight as possible.

Ma Bo Twisted Waist   **Right Gung Bo**

(81) From a twisted upper body position, (82) begin to shift into a (83) right gung bo position, (84) again with your right leg slightly bent and your left leg extended as straight as possible.

Ma Bo

(89) Move into a (90) ma bo stance by leading off with your right leg, followed by your left. (91) Then shift into a lau ma position by lifting your right leg and (92) rotating your body 90 degrees to the right.

Right Gung Bo **Ma Bo**

(77) Shift into a right gung bo position, this time with your right leg slightly bent and your left leg extended. (78) Return to (79) a ma bo position and then (80) twist your upper body to the left.

Ma Bo **Closed Horse**

(85) Shift to your left into a (86) ma bo position. (87) Bringing the right leg close to the left, (88) move into a closed horse stance, knees slightly bent.

Lau Ma **Ma Bo**

(93) Set your right foot down, locking your left knee against the back of your right leg. (94) Bend your knees as you (95) shift into a ma bo stance by (96) leading off with the left leg.

27

Gung Bo

From the ma bo position, (97) move to the right into a twisted upper body position. (98) Then shift to the left into a (99) gung bo stance, (100) with your left toes pointed inward toward the right.

Lau Ma   **Ma Bo**

(105) From the lau ma position, (106) shift into a ma bo stance by (107) leading off with the right leg and then (108) the left. Learn to cover as much distance as possible, maintaining a slight squat position at all times.

Ma Bo   **Modified Lau Ma**   **Ding Bo**

(113) Shift into a ma bo stance, then (114) a modified lau ma stance, crossing your right leg over the left. (115) Then pivot on your left foot into a (116) *ding bo* (cat) stance, with most of your weight on your back leg.

Ma Bo

(101) Shift to the right into a (102) ma bo stance, (103) then to the left into a lau ma position by (104) lifting the left foot and turning your body 90 degrees counterclockwise, your toes pointing toward the left.

Gung Bo

(109) Shift to the left into an upper body twisted position, keeping the lower body as stationary as possible and your feet immobile. (110) Begin to shift into a right gung bo stance with your legs slightly bent (111 & 112).

Ma Bo   **Gung Bo**

(117) Make a small circle counterclockwise with the right foot to shift into a (118) ma bo stance. (119) Shift to the left into an upper body twisted position and then (120) into a gung bo stance, your right leg bent.

Ma Bo   **Modified Lau Ma**

(121) From a ma bo stance, (122) shift into a modified lau ma stance by (123) crossing the left leg over the right and turning your head toward the right. (124) Lock your right knee against the back of the left leg.

Right Gung Bo   **Ma Bo**   **Closed Horse**

From an upper twisted body position, shift into the following: (129) a right gung bo, (130) a ma bo, and (131) a closed horse stance before (132) reverting to a ma bo by leading off with the right leg, followed by the left.

Right Gung Bo   **Left Gung Bo**

(137) From the right gung bo position, with right knee bent, (138) step into a (139) left gung bo and (140) back into a right gung bo by placing the left leg back. The right leg should remain stationary, knees slightly bent.

Ding Bo   **Ma Bo**

(125) Shift into a (126) ding bo, pivoting on the right foot and placing the left forward. (127) Draw a small circle clockwise with the left foot to shift into a ma bo. (128) Shift into an upper twisted body position.

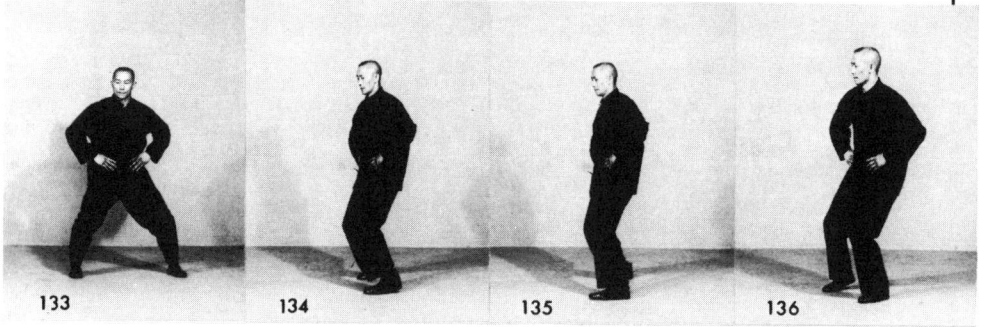

Ma Bo   **Left Gung Bo**

(133) Step forward with the left leg into a (134) left gung bo stance, (135) keeping the left knee bent and the right leg straight. (136) Prepare to step into a right gung bo position.

Right Gung Bo   **Left Gung Bo**

(141) From a right gung bo position, (142) shift into a left gung bo position by (143) placing your right foot back. (144) Bend the left knee as you are shifting.

Right Gung Bo   **Left Gung Bo**   **Ma Bo**

From a left gung bo position, (145) return to a right gung bo by placing the left foot back. (146) Revert to a left gung bo, and then (147) shift into a ma bo stance. (148) Bring your left foot into a closed horse stance.

Left Gung Bo   **Right Gung Bo**

From a twisted upper body position, (153) shift into a (154) left gung bo stance and then into a (155) right gung bo stance, keeping the right knee bent and the left leg straight. (156) Begin to shift into a ma bo stance.

Ma Bo   **Right Gung Bo**

(161) From a ma bo stance, (162) twist your upper body to the left, keeping the lower body stationary and your knees slightly bent. Then (163) shift into a (164) right gung bo position.

149   150   151   152

Closed Horse   Ma Bo

(149) From the closed horse stance, (150) lead off with your left foot, followed by the right, settling into a (151) ma bo position. (152) Twist into an upper body position by turning to the right.

157   158   159   160

Ma Bo   Closed Horse

(157) From the ma bo position, (158) shift into a closed horse stance by (159) placing the right foot next to the left. (160) Shift back into a ma bo stance by leading off with the right foot, followed by the left.

165   166   167   168

Ma Bo

(165) Shift into a (166) ma bo position with your weight evenly distributed on both feet. (167) Then sweep with the left foot, (168) stretching it out as far as possible. The right knee should remain bent.

Ma Bo

(169) From a left sweep position, (170) execute another sweep with the right foot, (171) keeping your left knee bent. (172) Shift into a ma bo position by leading off with the right leg, followed by the left.

Ma Bo   Ma Bo

(177) From the side ma bo position, (178) keep the left foot stationary as you (179) shift into a regular front ma bo position by placing the left foot back and (180) keeping the right foot stationary.

Ma Bo   Left Gung Bo

From a closed horse position, (185) shift into a regular ma bo and then into a (186) right upper body twisted position. (187) Shift into a left gung bo position, (188) with your left knee bent and your right leg straight.

Left Gung Bo   **Ma Bo**

(173) Turn to the right into a twisted upper body position, keeping the lower body stationary. (174) Turn into a left gung bo position and then (175) into a ma bo stance. (176) Begin to shift into a side ma bo position.

Left Gung Bo   **Ma Bo**   **Closed Horse**

(181) Shift into a right, upper body twisted position, but maintain a ma bo position below the waist. (182) Move into a left gung bo stance and then into a (183) ma bo stance before shifting into a (184) closed horse position.

Ma Bo   **Closed Horse**

(189) Shift into a (190) ma bo position and then (191) bring your left foot into a (192) closed horse stance, keeping your knees bent.

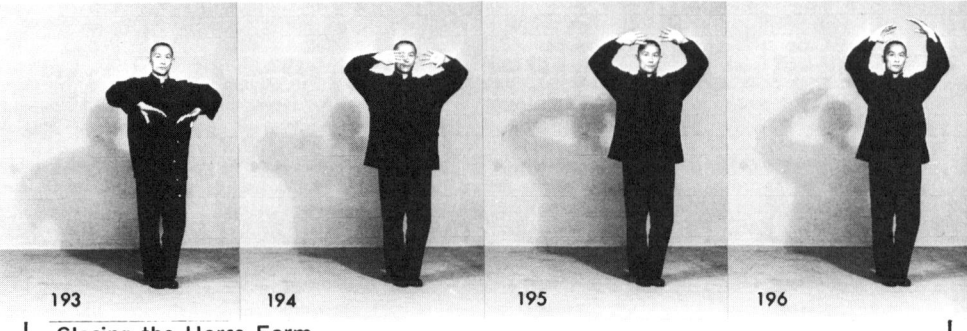

Closing the Horse Form

From a closed horse stance, (193) bring your hands up to (194) your face, simultaneously straightening your body to a standing position. (195) Turn your palms outward. (196) Begin to extend your hands forward.

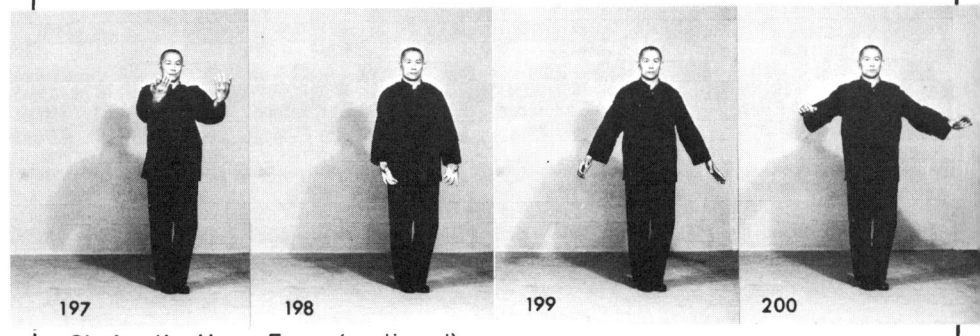

Closing the Horse Form (continued)

(197) Extend your hands forward in a circular downward motion. (198) Without stopping the movement, (199) begin to extend your arms outward (200) in a circular motion.

Closing the Horse Form (continued)

(201) Continue the circular motion until the right fist (202) touches the left open palm for the closing ceremony. (203) Drop your hands slowly to the sides to (204) complete the entire horse form.

Choy Lay Fut Exercises

The strength of the horse stance in free fighting is that it permits you to repel an aggressive attack and unbalance your opponent without giving ground yourself. Of the following exercises, the first two are designed to improve your power and stability in the horse stance introduced in the preceding chapter.

The purpose of the first exercise is to increase your leg power

Assume the ma bo position and grip the end of a pole (approximately 1½" in diameter) with your hands about two feet apart. With your partner similarly situated, try to unbalance or move each other backward without poking or using jerky motions. Keep the pushing smooth and continuous, with both feet on the floor and the legs in a half-squatting position. Movement should be constant, not bouncing up and down.

and your sensitivity to balance in the feet. The second exercise teaches one of Kung-Fu's most basic concepts: always give with an opponent. When he pushes, pull with him; when he pulls, push with him. Both of the first two exercises should help you develop sensitivity to an opponent's strength.

Well-coordinated blocking is vital to successful execution of the Cheung Kune form to be introduced in the following chapter. The three star blocking exercise below will help put rhythm in your blocking and will toughen your arms against hard kicks and punches.

Push-Pull Exercise

(1) Place your left arm against your partner's arm, making contact at the wrist. (2) When one partner pushes, (3) the other grasps his arm and pulls, being careful not to lose balance himself. (4-7) Take turns pushing and pulling in a continuous motion. The object is to pull or push your opponent off balance without sacrificing your own equilibrium. Keep your body firm but not stiff.

Blocking Exercise

(1 & 2) Execute an inward block in unison with your partner. Then, still in unison, (3-5) switch to an outward block without breaking rhythm. (6 & 7) In a continuous motion, turn the outward blocks into lower outward blocks. (8 & 9) Maintaining your rhythm, perform the same blocking sequence with the opposite arm. Execute the blocking motions slowly and softly until you have mastered the pattern; blocking too hard too soon will result in bruised arms.

Elemental Aid to Cheung Kune

This section is included to give more detail to some of the most recurring movements in the cheung kune form which follows.

Inward Block

To execute a left inward block, (1) stand with your hands at waist level (palms down and fingers pointing toward each other) and your feet together, knees slightly bent. (2) Raise your left hand vertically as you retract your right hand to the side. (3) Block by moving your elbow toward the right. Reverse the hand positions for a right inward block.

Finger Throat Jab (Bul Jee)

To execute a right finger throat jab, (1) step to the right with your right foot (2) into a ma bo stance, simultaneously moving both hands to the right in a slight arc. (3) The right hand swings upward toward the target as the left hand moves in the opposite direction toward the waist.

2

3

2

3

45

Eagle Beak Block

To execute an eagle beak block, (1) stand in a ready position with your right arm extended, fist facing forward, and your left clenched fist at your hip. Your head should be turned to the right. (2) Using primarily wrist action, (3) rotate the right hand in a counterclockwise movement, (4) the fingers extended and the thumb tucked in. (5) As you complete the rotation of your hand, (6) shift your weight to the right into a gung bo stance to prepare yourself for a corkscrew punch.

1.

4

2

3

5

6

Corkscrew Punch

To execute a corkscrew punch, (1) stand in a gung bo position with your right arm extended, fist clenched, and your left clenched fist placed at your hip. Your head should face the right. (2) As you lower your right fist, (3) simultaneously twist and punch forward with the left fist, (4) twisting it inward as you deliver the punch.

Slice Block

To execute a slice block, (1) stand in a gung bo stance with your right clenched fist raised over your left arm. (2) Slice the right fist over the left as you simultaneously move into a ma bo stance by shifting your weight to the left. (3) The block is completed when (4) both arms are outstretched to the sides.

Back Fist

To execute a back fist strike, (1) swing your left arm to the left in a large arc by (2) twisting your upper body in that direction. (3) At the same time, raise your right hand high and (4) deliver the back fist punch by striking downward to the target.

Double Vertical Block

To execute a double vertical block, (1) stand in a ma bo stance with your arms outstretched, fists clenched. (2) Draw your hands in toward your waist—fingers outstretched as if to pick up a large bundle. (3) Raise your hands toward your face, (4) then twist them outward—palms facing each other.

Circular Block and Scrape Punch

To execute a circular block and scrape punch, (1) swing both open hands downward and (2) toward your left in a circular motion until (3) your left clenched fist is over your head and your right hand is at your chest. (4) Simultaneously twist your hips to the right into a lau ma position. (5) Punch downward and (6) forward with your left fist, (7) as you raise your right open hand to protect your head or to counter.

2

3

6

7

Upper Block and Uppercut

To execute an upper block and left uppercut punch, (1) squat in a lau ma stance with your right arm (fist clenched) extended downward and your left open hand protecting your head. (2) Bring both hands to your left, (3) extending your left arm straight out and your right hand to your left hip. (4) Step forward with your right foot into a gung bo stance, simultaneously clenching your left fist. (5) Swing both hands forward and upward in a circular motion. (6) Your right hand moves higher to protect your head (7) while your left hand applies the uppercut.

Single Flying Foot Kick

To execute a single flying foot kick, (1) stand in a closed horse stance, with the right hand crossing the left. (2) Raise your right foot and (3) kick with a snapping motion. Contact is made with the outward edge of the foot.

Vertical Punch

(4) After executing the flying kick, (5) shift into a ma bo stance, both hands held at waist level. (6) Then thrust your right hand forward to execute the vertical punch, simultaneously moving your left fist backward. Twist your hip sharply toward the left as you deliver the punch.

57

Side Block

To execute a side block, (1) stand in a right ma bo position. (2) Cross your right elbow in front of your body toward the left and (3) your right foot over your left. (4) Your right hand continues in a circular movement as (5) you bend your knees into a lau ma stance.

2

3

5

Haymaker

To execute a haymaker, (1) stand in a left lau ma stance. (2) Raise your left hand and (3) block downward in front of your body. (4) Then twist your body to the left—your right hand trailing. (5) Step back slightly with your left foot and (6) deliver the haymaker. The pivoting of your body gives an extra thrust to the delivery of the punch.

1

4

2

3

5

6

61

Lower Block

To execute a lower block, (1) chop down with the right fist as you (2) place your weight on your left foot and (3) simultaneously raise your left open hand into an upper block position.

Tiger Claw

To execute a tiger claw from another technique, (1) shift into a gung bo stance and (2) swing both hands in an upward arc. (3) Claw with one hand going forward and the other blocking downward.

2

3

2

3

63

Double-Hand Horizontal Block

To execute a double-hand horizontal block, (1) shift into a (2) lau ma position with (3) both hands by your waist. (4) Then, simultaneously move your hands to the left.

Left-Right Elbow Blocks

To execute left and right elbow blocks, (1) hold your left hand upright, aligned with your shoulder, and your right hand approximately at waist level, palm down. (2) Abruptly move your left elbow to the right, simultaneously swinging your right hand down to your side. (3) Reverse hand positions for the (4) right elbow block.

Foot Sweep

To execute a foot sweep, (1) hold your right hand high over your head. (2) Slice it over your left as you pivot your left foot. (3) The slicing and sweeping occur simultaneously, and (4) both movements end at the same time.

CHEUNG KUNE
The Long Range Fist of Choy Lay Fut

All movements in the following section should be executed smoothly and with continuity. They should not be rigid, but firm. The emphasis on inhaling and exhaling is important.

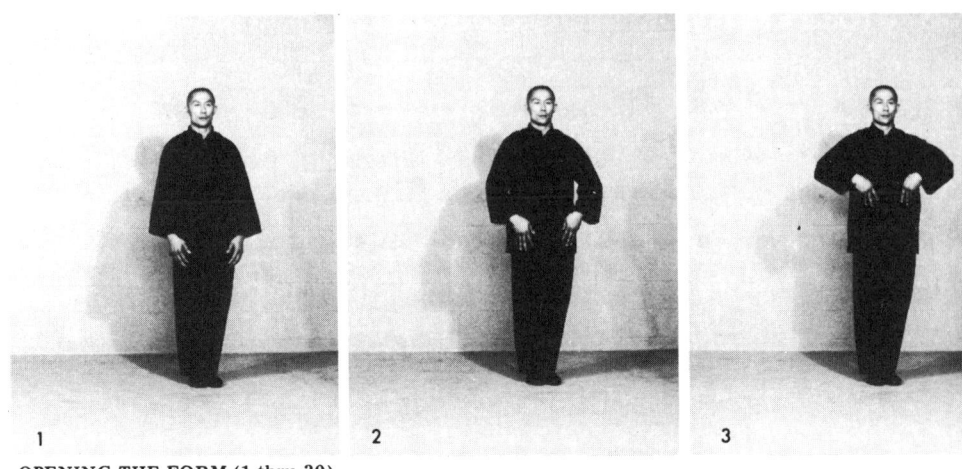

OPENING THE FORM (1 thru 30)

(1) Stand at attention with your feet together and arms at your sides. (2) Begin to raise your hands by drawing your elbows up. (3) Breathe in as you slowly raise your hands toward your face.

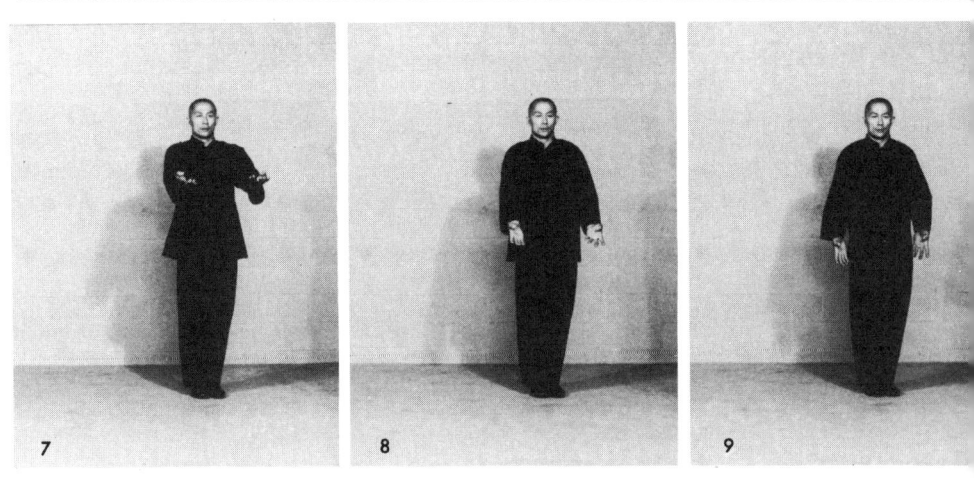

(7) With your palms still facing upward, continue to lower your hands (8) until they are (9) at your sides. Note: Your thumbs are tucked in as you do this movement.

(4) Breathe out as you (5) begin to turn your hands forward and downward. (6) With palms facing upward, lower your hands.

(10) Slowly raise your hands—palms up—toward your ears as you breathe in. (11) Begin to turn your hands before they reach your face so that (12) both palms face the floor.

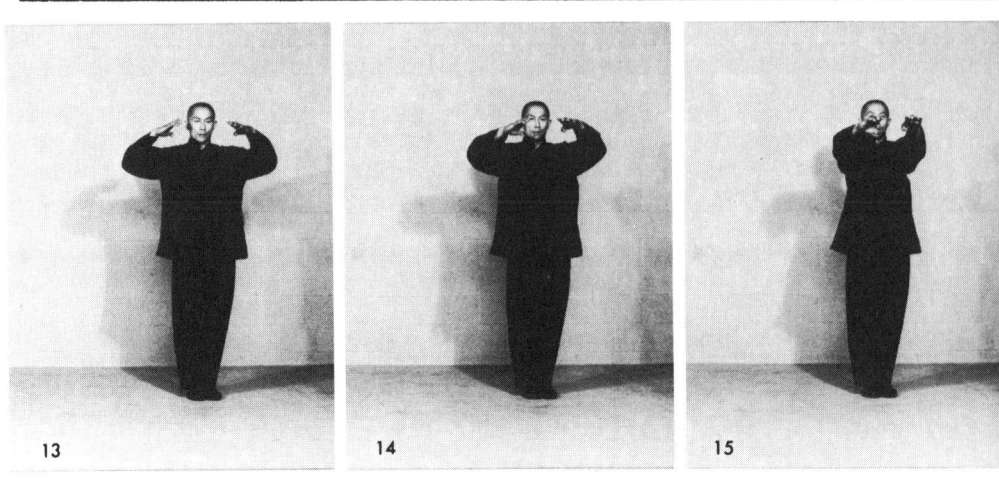

(13) With your elbows at shoulder level, (14) breathe out as you simultaneously thrust both arms forward (15) with your palms facing the floor.

(19) From the outstretched arm position, (20) begin to bring your hands (21) together so the palms face each other.

(16) Then breathe in as you (17) spread both arms out to your sides at (18) shoulder level, forming a "T". Your body should be kept immobile during these movements.

(22) Cross your right hand over your left, simultaneously bending your knees slightly. (23) Your crossed hands should be in front of your face before (24) you drop them to waist level and toward the sides.

(25) From their sides, (26) spread your arms, raising them slightly above your waist before you begin to move your hands in a circular motion. (27) Your arms are at chest level.

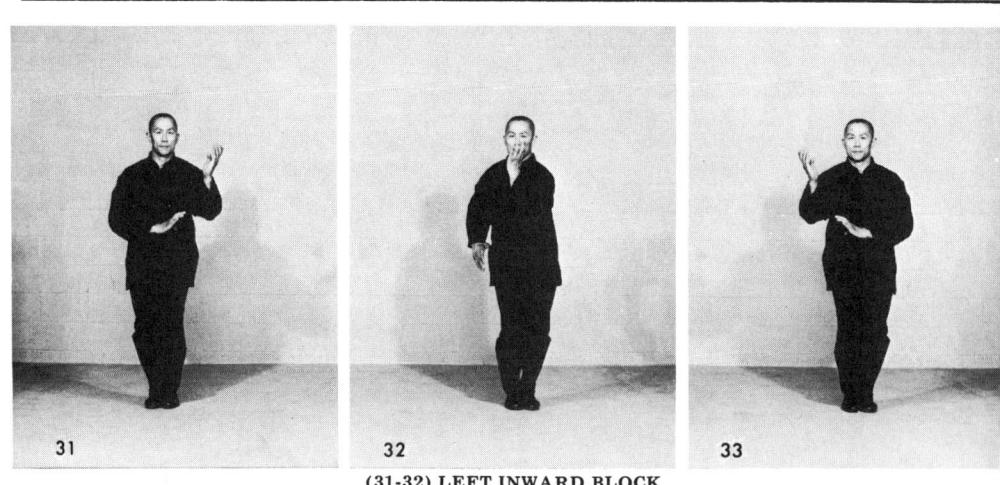

(31-32) LEFT INWARD BLOCK

(31) With your right hand protecting your body, execute a left inward block by raising your left hand vertically and (32) moving it toward your right. (33) Prepare a right inward block by reversing the hand positions.

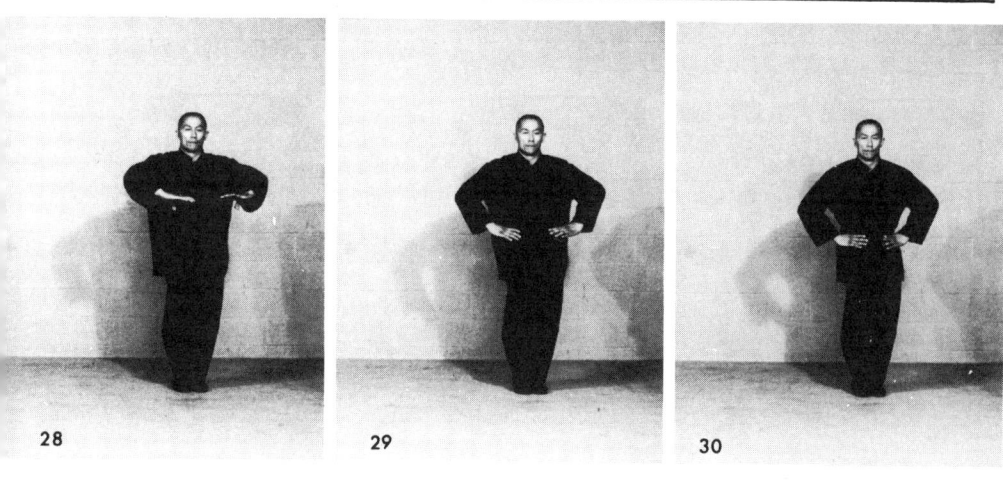

(28) Continue the movement as your fingers point toward each other and you begin to lower your hands. (29) Lower your hands (30) to your waist.

33-34) RIGHT INWARD BLOCK

(34) Execute the right inward block by moving your right arm toward your left. (35) Then step to the right as you move both hands in a circular arc, (36) preparing for a right finger throat jab as you shift into a ma bo.

(35-37) FINGER JAB

(37) After executing a finger jab, (38) make a counterclockwise, circular eagle beak block with the right hand, (39) simultaneously moving into a gung bo position—your fist clenched palm upward.

(42-44) CORKSCREW PUNCH

(43) After executing the eagle beak block, (44) execute a corkscrew punch by twisting the left fist clockwise. (45) Then prepare a slice block by raising your right hand.

(38-41) EAGLE BEAK BLOCK

(40) The block is executed primarily by the wrist motion, the fingers pointing downward. (41) The purpose of the block is to trap an opponent's punch and (42) divert his energy away from you.

(45-48) SLICE BLOCK

(46) Slice your right hand over your left (47) as you shift into a ma bo stance. The right arm continues to slice until it is extended to the side, (48) while the left arm simultaneously moves in the opposite direction.

(51) CLOSED HORSE STANCE

(49) From an outstretched position, (50) shift into a (51) closed horse stance by drawing the right foot to your left and placing your left fist on the hip. Continue to look over your right shoulder.

(54-57) EAGLE BEAK BLOCK

(55) Execute the eagle beak block by (56) turning your right open hand (57) counterclockwise, retaining the ma bo stance and still looking to your right. Your left clenched fist should remain on your hip.

(53) MA BO STANCE

(52) Step off with your right foot to (53) shift into a ma bo stance. (54) Once your position is set, start to move your right hand into an eagle beak position.

(58-60) CORKSCREW PUNCH

(58) Then withdraw the right hand to your side as (59) you prepare to deliver a (60) left-hand corkscrew punch, at the same time moving into a gung bo stance.

After executing the corkscrew punch from the gung bo position, (61) prepare a slice block by raising your right hand and (62) slicing it downward and over the left arm. (63) Simultaneously shift into a ma bo stance.

(67) CLOSED HORSE STANCE   **(69) MA BO STANCE**

(67) After moving into the closed horse stance, repeat Steps 51-67 two times before continuing with the next. (68) Lead off with your right foot into a (69) ma bo position.

(61-64) SLICE BLOCK

(64) Simultaneously continue the slicing motion of the right arm and extend the left arm in the opposite direction. (65) Bring the left fist to your hip and (66) the right leg in as you prepare to move into a closed horse stance.

(70) Balance your body as you (71) begin an eagle beak block (72) by rotating your right hand at the wrist in a counterclockwise circle.

(70-74) EAGLE BEAK BLOCK

(73) As you complete the eagle beak block, (74) prepare to deliver a corkscrew punch by (75) withdrawing your blocking hand to the side and thrusting your left hand forward.

(78-81) SLICE BLOCK

After delivering the corkscrew punch, (79) execute a slice block by slicing the right arm over the left as you (80) automatically shift into a ma bo stance and (81) extend both arms outward.

(75-77) CORKSCREW PUNCH

(76) Keep your body immobile as you deliver a left punch, (77) twisting it clockwise as it is fully extended. (78) At the same time, snap your hips into a gung bo stance.

(82) Execute an eagle beak block with your right hand as (83) you return your left fist to your hip (84) in a ready position, always facing your imaginary opponent.

(82-86) EAGLE BEAK BLOCK

(85) After completing the eagle beak block, (86) prepare to deliver a left corkscrew punch, (87) snapping your hips into a gung bo stance as you deliver the punch.

(89-92) BACK FIST

While you are moving into a left gung bo, (91) raise your right hand high to the side of your head. (92) Apply a back fist punch to (93) the opponent's temple. All movements should be performed in a continuous motion.

(87-88) CORKSCREW PUNCH

(88) As soon as the punch is completed, (89) twist your body toward the front, (90) swinging the left arm in a semi-arc direction as you begin to shift into a left gung bo position.

(93-96) SLICE BLOCK

(94) Execute a slice block by slicing the left hand over the right, (95) automatically shifting into a ma bo stance. (96) Then begin to return the right fist to your hip.

(98) CLOSED HORSE STANCE

(97) From a ma bo stance, (98) shift into a closed horse stance by bringing the left leg next to the right, leaving the left arm extended. (99) Then begin to shift into a ma bo stance by leading off with the left foot.

(101-104) EAGLE BEAK BLOCK

(103) Continue the eagle beak movement from your waist until (104) your fingers are facing downward. (105) Then begin a right corkscrew punch by snapping your hips into a gung bo position.

(100) MA BO STANCE

(100) Balance yourself, and with your right fist still on your hip, (101) begin a left eagle beak block (102) in a circular clockwise motion with your left hand.

05-106) CORKSCREW PUNCH

(106) As you twist your right wrist inward into the punch, (107) raise your left hand high by the left side of your face, (108) and prepare to deliver a slice block.

(107-110) SLICE BLOCK

(109) Execute the slice block as you (110) retract your right fist to your hip and extend your blocking arm. (111) Leave your left arm extended as you bring the left leg into a closed horse stance.

(115) From the ma bo position, spread the fingers of your left hand, keeping only the thumb tucked in. (116) Execute a circular eagle beak block by (117) rotating your hand in a clockwise motion.

(112) CLOSED HORSE STANCE   **(114) MA BO STANCE**

(112) From a closed horse position, (113) spread your left leg until you are in a (114) ma bo position, balancing yourself, with your right fist on your hip and your left hand still extended.

115-118) EAGLE BEAK BLOCK   **(119-120) CORKSCREW PUNCH**

(118) After executing the beak block, (119) deliver a right corkscrew punch by snapping your hips into a gung bo stance and (120) simultaneously punching and twisting your fist as you retract the left hand to your side.

(121) After executing the corkscrew punch, raise your left hand to your head. (122) Execute a slice block by slicing your left hand over the right. (123) At the same time, return your right hand to your hip.

(125-128) EAGLE BEAK BLOCK

(127) Execute the eagle beak block. (128) Most of the movement should come from the wrist. (129) As soon as the block is completed, snap your hips into a gung bo stance in preparation for a corkscrew punch.

(121-124) SLICE BLOCK

(124) With your left arm extended, (125) rotate your hand in a clockwise motion as you simultaneously return to a ma bo stance. (126) Extend your fingers (thumb tucked in) in preparation for the circular eagle beak block.

(129-130) CORKSCREW PUNCH   **(131-132) CIRCULAR BLOCK**

(130) Execute the corkscrew punch by simultaneously twisting and punching with the right fist. (131) Execute a right circular block and back fist strike by (132) turning your head to the right and blocking in a downward motion.

(133) BACK FIST STRIKE

(133) Follow the right circular block by striking your imaginary opponent's temple with a left back fist. (134) Execute a slice block with the right arm while (135) shifting into a ma bo stance—your arms in front of your chest.

(140) MA BO STANCE

(139) From a closed horse stance, lead off with the right leg into a (140) ma bo stance, still facing in the same direction. (141) Then begin a circular eagle beak block as your feet come to a complete stop—in balance.

(134-136) SLICE BLOCK **(138) CLOSED HORSE STANCE**

(136) Stretch your arms out forcefully, (137) then retract your left fist to your hip in a ready position, (138) keeping the right hand extended as you bring your left leg into a closed horse position.

(141-144) EAGLE BEAK BLOCK

(142) Make a circular counterclockwise motion with the right hand, remembering to use primarily wrist action, (143) until you have completed the block. (144) You are still faced in the same direction, in a ma bo stance.

(145) As soon as the eagle beak block is completed, snap your hips into a gung bo stance. (146) Retract your right arm to the side and (147) begin a left corkscrew punch.

(149-153) SLICE BLOCK

(151) As you execute the slice block, (152) both of your hands continue to spread out and (153) you automatically move into a ma bo position with your arms outstretched.

(145-148) CORKSCREW PUNCH

(148) Execute the corkscrew punch by simultaneously twisting and punching with the left fist. (149) Raise your right hand to prepare for a slice block, (150) then begin the block by slicing the right arm over the left.

(154-156) DOUBLE-HAND VERTICAL BLOCK

(154) Prepare to execute a vertical, double-hand block by drawing your hands toward your waist—fingers outstretched as if to pick up a large bundle. (155) Raise your hands toward your face and (156) twist them outward.

(157-159) RIGHT CIRCULAR BLOCK

From a double-hand block, (157) move both hands to your right, then swing them downward and (158) toward your left in a circular motion (159) until your left hand is over your head and your right hand is at your chest.

(160-163) LEFT SCRAPING PUNCH

(163) By the time your left hand reaches the downward swing, your right hand should be over your head. (164) Lead off with the left foot into a (165) gung bo, keeping your left hand continuously moving in a left upper block.

(160) Prepare for a left scraping punch by (161) twisting your body toward a lau ma position and punching downward and forward with your left fist. (162) Your right open hand should be in an upper block position.

(164-167) LEFT UPPER BLOCK AND RIGHT UPPERCUT PUNCH

(166) From the upswing, simultaneously sweep both hands down and toward your left in a large arc. (167) Execute a right uppercut punch (168) as you move into a ma bo position to prepare for a left slice block.

(168-170) SLICE BLOCK

(169) As you execute the slice block, (170) both of your hands continue to spread out to the sides and you automatically move into a ma bo position with your arms outstretched. (171) Begin to draw both hands inward.

(174-175) LEFT CIRCULAR BLOCK **(176-177) RIGHT SCRAPING PUNCH**

(175) To execute a left circular block, swing both hands downward and toward your right in a circular motion. (176) After completing the upswing, (177) execute a scraping punch as you move into a lau ma stance.

(171-173) DOUBLE-HAND VERTICAL BLOCK

(172) Prepare a vertical, double-hand block by continuing to draw both hands in toward your waist—fingers outstretched as if to pick up a large bundle. (173) Raise both hands toward your face, (174) twisting them to the left.

(178) From the lau ma, scraping punch position, execute a sweeping, right-hand upper block by (179) sweeping the right open hand upward and across your body as you (180) lead off with the right leg into a gung bo stance.

**(178-183) RIGHT UPPER BLOC(K)
AND LEFT UPPERCUT PUNC(H)**

(181) As you build momentum for a forward, right-hand sweep, (182) prepare to execute a left-hand uppercut by (183) thrusting your left fist upward. Your right hand is still raised over your head.

(184-187) SLICE BLOCK

(187) From the outstretched position, (188) execute an eagle beak block by rotating your wrist counterclockwise, (189) simultaneously returning the left fist to your hip.

(184) After performing the uppercut, prepare to execute a slice block by (185) slicing your right hand over your left as you move into a ma bo stance. (186) Both hands continue their motion until the arms are outstretched.

(8-190) EAGLE BEAK BLOCK

(190) After completing the eagle beak block, (191) lower your right fist and (192) snap into a gung bo stance, preparing to deliver a corkscrew punch.

(191-193) CORKSCREW PUNCH

(193) After delivering the corkscrew punch, (194) prepare a slice block by raising your right hand and slicing it downward and over the left arm, (195) simultaneously shifting into a ma bo stance.

(197-199) DOUBLE-HAND VERTICAL BLOCK

(199) As soon as you raise your hands to your face, twist them outward and to your right. (200) Then swing both hands downward and toward your left in a circular motion (201) until the upswing is completed.

(194-196) SLICE BLOCK

(196) Continue the slicing motion of the right arm and extend the left arm in the opponent's direction. (197) Then execute a vertical, double-hand block by drawing both hands in toward your waist (198) and up toward your face.

(200-203) LEFT PALM-EDGE STRIKE

(202) Pivot to the right into a lau ma stance and (203) execute a left, palm-edge strike by exerting left-hand force downward as your right hand executes an upward block. (204) Begin to move into a ma bo stance.

(204-207) LEFT DOWNWARD BLOCK AND RIGHT SCRAPING FIST

(205) With arms outstretched, (206) thrust both hands toward each other—the right executing a scraping roundhouse punch and the left a downward block—as you (207) move the left foot to the right while squatting lower.

(209-211) SINGLE FLYING FOOT KICK

(211) The single flying kick is executed with a snapping motion. Contact is made with the outward edge of the foot. (212) After the kick, (213) position yourself in a ma bo stance.

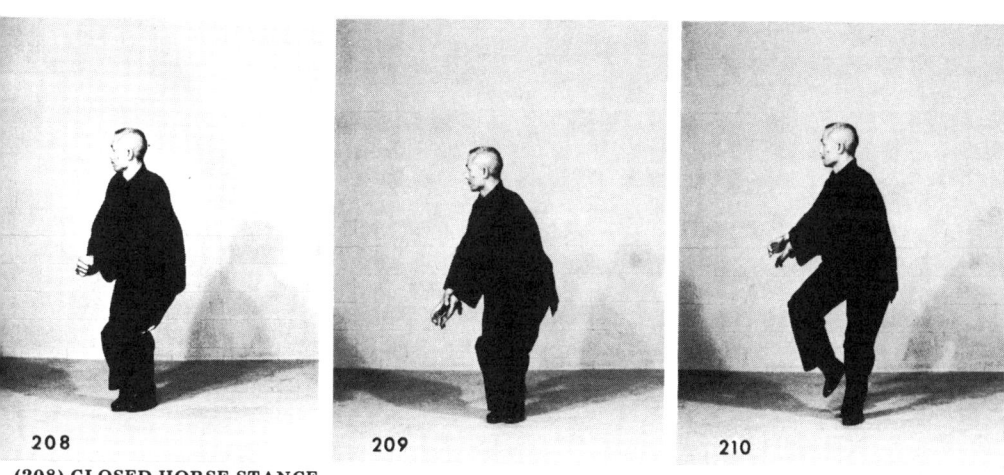

(208) CLOSED HORSE STANCE

(208) Continue to move your hands until (209) the right hand crosses over the left, simultaneously shifting into a closed horse stance (210) in preparation for a flying kick.

(212-214) VERTICAL PUNCH

(214) Then thrust out a vertical punch and (215) withdraw the right hand to your hip. (216) Execute an eagle beak block by rotating your wrist counterclockwise in a circular motion.

(215-217) EAGLE BEAK BLOCK

(217) After executing the eagle beak block, (218) deliver a left-hand corkscrew punch, (219) simultaneously shifting into a gung bo stance and withdrawing your right hand to the side.

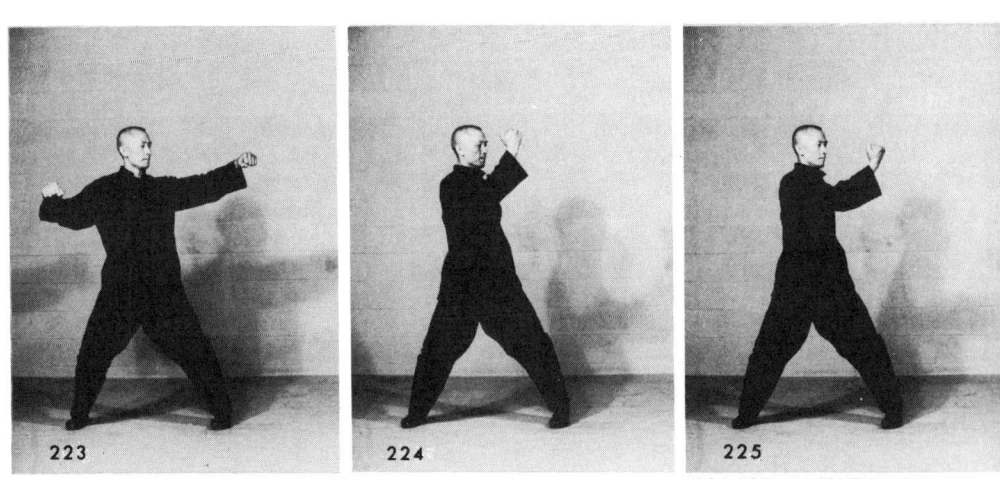

(221-223) LEFT CIRCULAR BLOCK　　　　　　　　　**(224-225) BACK FIST STRIKE**

(223) While you are moving into a left gung bo position, (224) raise your right hand high to the side of your head. (225) Then apply a back fist strike.

(218-220) CORKSCREW PUNCH

(220) As soon as the punch is completed, (221) twist your body toward the left, (222) swinging the left arm in a semi-arc direction as you begin to shift into a left gung bo position.

(226-227) LEFT INWARD BLOCK

(226) Prepare to execute a left inward block by raising your left hand vertically. (227) Then twist your hips slightly to the right as you block with your left elbow. (228) Prepare to execute a lau ma side block.

(228-229) RIGHT INWARD BLOCK

(229) Execute a right, lau ma side block by crossing your right elbow over your face toward the left and (230) your right foot over the left. (231) Your right hand continues its movement toward your left in a downward arc.

(233-235) LEFT CIRCULAR BLOCK

(235) Continue pivoting your body counterclockwise, using your leading left hand to block. (236) Your right hand, preparing for the haymaker, follows your body, (237) which is moving into a gung bo stance.

(230-232) LAU MA SIDE BLOCK

(232) After the completion of the downward swing, (233) begin to pivot your body toward the left, (234) raising your left hand above your head to block.

(236-238) HAYMAKER FIST

(238) Pivoting your body gives extra thrust to the delivery of the haymaker. (239) Step back with your left foot into a lau ma stance, (240) simultaneously withdrawing your right hand and extending your left hand forward.

**(239-241) LAU MA
OPEN-HAND BLOCK**

(241) Bring your right hand to the side of your head, and block with the open left hand. (242) Execute an eagle beak block by rotating your hand clockwise, and (243) prepare for a thrust punch.

(246-248) BACK FIST STRIKE   **(249) LEFT OPEN-HAND BLOCK**

(247) Execute a right, back fist strike as your body faces the left. (248) The striking fist should twist slightly in its downward swing so the knuckles face the floor. (249) Twist your body to the right for an open-hand block.

**(242-245) EAGLE BEAK BLOCK
AND THRUST PUNCH**

(244) Step slightly forward with the right foot (245) into a ma bo position as you deliver the thrust punch, returning your left hand to your chest for protection. (246) Then turn your body to the left for a back fist strike.

RIGHT OPEN-HAND BLOCK

(250) Execute a right, open-hand block and continue your motion (251) into a right-hand, horizontal block as you (252) simultaneously shift into a lau ma stance by crossing the right foot over the left.

(253) LAU MA STANCE

(253) The block is made with your hands and body moving in opposite directions. (254) After performing the right-hand horizontal block, execute a left horizontal block by (255) pivoting to your left.

(259-260) SINGLE FLYING KICK AND FINGER THRUST

(259) Execute a left, single-flying kick by snapping your left leg out, (260) and simultaneously strike out with a right finger thrust. (261) Keep your balance when performing this technique.

(254-256) LEFT HORIZONTAL BLOCK

(257-258) CIRCULAR BLOCK

(256) After pivoting 180 degrees to the left into a ma bo stance, (257) pivot to your right (258) into a lau ma stance.

(261-262) VERTICAL PUNCH

(262) Execute a left vertical punch as you simultaneously shift into a ma bo stance. (263) Then begin an eagle beak block, (264) making a clockwise circle with your left hand.

(263-265) EAGLE BEAK BLOCK **(266-267) CORKSCREW PUNCH**

(265) After the block, (266) return your left hand to your side as you shift into a gung bo stance, (267) simultaneously executing a corkscrew punch.

(270-272) LEFT CIRCULAR BLOCK

(271) Continue the movements of the circular block, bringing your left arm up (272) to protect the upper part of your body and (273) the right arm down to protect the lower portion.

(268-269) RIGHT CIRCULAR BLOCK

(268) Execute a circular block—vertical punch combination by (269) swinging your right arm in a clockwise (your left to right) circular motion. (270) At the same time circle your left arm counterclockwise (your right to left).

(273-276) VERTICAL PUNCH

(274) Continue the circular right and left hand blocks several times before (275) delivering a vertical left hand punch. (276) The right arm should be in a vertical blocking position to protect your head.

(277-279) LEFT CIRCULAR BLOCK

(277) After delivery of the vertical punch, (278) execute circular blocks with both hands, (279) the left hand circling clockwise and the right counterclockwise. As your right hand moves downward, your left hand moves upward.

(283-285) VERTICAL PUNCH

(283) From a gung bo stance, (284) execute a vertical punch as soon as you are in balance. (285) The left hand should be in a vertical blocking position to protect your head.

(280-282) RIGHT CIRCULAR BLOCK

(280) Keep circling your hands in wide arcs with precise timing, (281) and after several complete circles, (282) step out with the left leg into a gung bo stance.

(286-287) RIGHT CIRCULAR BLOCK

(286) After the right vertical punch, (287) make a circular block—right arm moving downward in a clockwise (your left to right) motion and (288) left arm going upward in a counterclockwise (your right to left) motion.

(288-291) LEFT CIRCULAR BLOCK

(289) Continue to execute the left-right circular blocks, (290) moving your arms in opposite directions with good timing. (291) As your left hand goes upward, your right hand should move downward.

(292-295) VERTICAL PUNCH

(295) Deliver the punch. (296) Then execute a lower block by chopping down with the right fist, (297) drawing the right foot back into a gung bo stance as you bring the left open hand into an upper block position.

(292) After executing the circular blocks a number of times, (293) step out with your left foot into a gung bo stance. (294) Simultaneously bring right hand up in a vertical block position in preparation for a left vertical punch.

(296-298) RIGHT LOWER BLOCK

(298) Alternate the blocking technique by (299) shifting your left foot into a gung bo position. (300) Execute a left lower block by chopping down with your left fist. Your right open hand protects your head.

(299-302) LEFT LOWER BLOCK

(301 & 302) After executing the left lower block, (303) prepare to execute a right lower block by chopping down with your right fist as you raise your left hand, simultaneously moving your right foot back.

**(305-308) EAGLE BEAK BLOCK
AND CORKSCREW PUNCH**

(307) As soon as you have performed the eagle beak block, (308) execute a right corkscrew punch by twisting and punching. (309) Then immediately shift to the right in preparation for a left back fist strike.

(303-304) RIGHT LOWER BLOCK

(304) As you execute a right lower block, your left hand should be positioned in an upper block and your body in a gung bo stance. (305 & 306) Execute an eagle beak block.

(309-311) BACK FIST STRIKE

(310) Lead off with your right hand in a circular blocking motion and (311) follow up with a left back fist punch. (312) Prepare to execute a slice block by slicing the right hand over the left.

(312-314) SLICE BLOCK

(313) As you complete the slice block, move into a ma bo position, (314) stretching your arms to the sides. (315) Bring your left fist to the hip as you prepare to move into a closed horse stance.

(319-321) EAGLE BEAK BLOCK

(319) Execute an eagle beak block by (320) rotating your right wrist inward. (321) As soon as you've executed the eagle beak block, prepare for a left corkscrew punch.

316
(316) CLOSED HORSE STANCE

(316) Shift into a closed horse stance by bringing the right foot to your left. (317) Then begin to shift into a (318) ma bo stance as you prepare for an eagle beak block—keeping your right hand extended.

(322-323) CORKSCREW PUNCH

(322) Retract your right fist to the hip as you twist your hips into a gung bo stance, (323) simultaneously executing a left corkscrew punch. (324) Block with your left hand just prior to moving into a low horse stance.

(324-327) LOW HORSE VERTICAL PUNCH

(325) In one continuous movement, (326) drop toward the floor, (327) your right knee barely meeting the floor. Your left hand protects your upper body as you apply the vertical punch from a low horse stance.

(331) TIGER CLAW

(331) Execute the tiger claw as you raise your body slightly by drawing your left foot in. (332) From a semi-low horse stance, execute a left eagle beak block, (333) rotating your wrist clockwise.

(328-330) EAGLE BEAK BLOCK

(328) After applying the vertical punch, remain in a low horse stance and (329) execute an eagle beak block by rotating your right wrist counterclockwise. (330) Prepare to execute a left tiger claw.

(332-335) EAGLE BEAK BLOCK

(334) Just as you are about to complete the eagle beak block, (335) draw your right hand to your hip and (336) slide your right foot back. Your left hand protects your body as you deliver a straight right punch.

(336-337) STRAIGHT PUNCH

(337) After executing the straight right punch, (338) simultaneously swing both hands toward your left as you (339) automatically shift into a ma bo stance.

(338-343) RIGHT UPPER BLOCK AND LEFT UPPERCUT PUNCH

(343) After unleashing the left uppercut punch, (344) execute a slice block, slicing the right hand over the left and (345) simultaneously moving into a ma bo position.

(340) From the ma bo stance, (341) execute a sweeping, right hand upper block as you shift into a gung bo position, (342) preparing to unleash a left hand uppercut.

(344-346) SLICE BLOCK

(346) Continue to spread both hands out. (347) Then bring your left hand to your hip as you (348) shift into a closed horse stance, moving your right foot to your left.

(349) CLOSED HORSE STANCE

(349) From a closed horse position, (350) spread your right foot until (351) you are in a ma bo position, with your right hand still extended and your left hand on your hip.

(355-357) CORKSCREW PUNCH

(355) After executing the eagle beak block, (356) deliver a left corkscrew punch by snapping your hips into a gung bo stance, (357) simultaneously punching and twisting your fist as you retract your left hand to the side.

(351-354) EAGLE BEAK BLOCK

(352) From the ma bo position, (353) execute a circular eagle beak block by rotating your right hand in a counterclockwise motion. (354) The fingers of your right hand should be spread, with only the thumb tucked in.

(358) After delivery of the corkscrew punch, (359) prepare to execute a combination slice block—foot sweep technique by (360) pivoting on your left foot and slicing your right hand over your left.

127

(358-363) FOOT SWEEP AND SLICE BLOCK

(361) As your right hand is slicing, your right foot is simultaneously sweeping, (362) and both movements end at the same time. (363) The left foot should be kept low and the right foot light and extended.

(367-369) EAGLE BEAK BLOCK

(367) With your left fist on your hip, (368) execute an eagle beak block by (369) rotating your left hand clockwise.

(364-366) FOOT SWEEP AND SLICE BLOCK

(364) After completion of the right slice block—foot sweep combination, (365) execute a left combination by slicing the left hand over the right, (366) at the same time sweeping the left foot.

(370) CORKSCREW PUNCH   **(371-372) BACK FIST STRIKE**

(370) Deliver a right corkscrew punch and (371) execute a right circular block by turning your head to the right. (372) Follow up with a left back fist strike.

(373-374) SLICE BLOCK

After execution of the back fist strike, (373 & 374) make a right slice block by simultaneously slicing your right hand downward and over your left arm. (375) Begin to move your right foot to your left into a closed horse stance.

(379-380) CORKSCREW PUNCH

(379) After execution of the eagle beak block, deliver a left corkscrew punch by (380 & 381) snapping into a gung bo stance and simultaneously punching and twisting the left hand inward.

(376) CLOSED HORSE STANCE   **(378) EAGLE BEAK BLOCK**

(376) From the closed horse stance, (377) shift into a ma bo position by stepping off with your right foot. (378) Then execute a right eagle beak block by rotating your hand counterclockwise.

(381-384) SLICE BLOCK

(382) Perform a slice block by (383) slicing the right hand over the left arm, (384) simultaneously shifting into a ma bo stance as your arms are extended out fully.

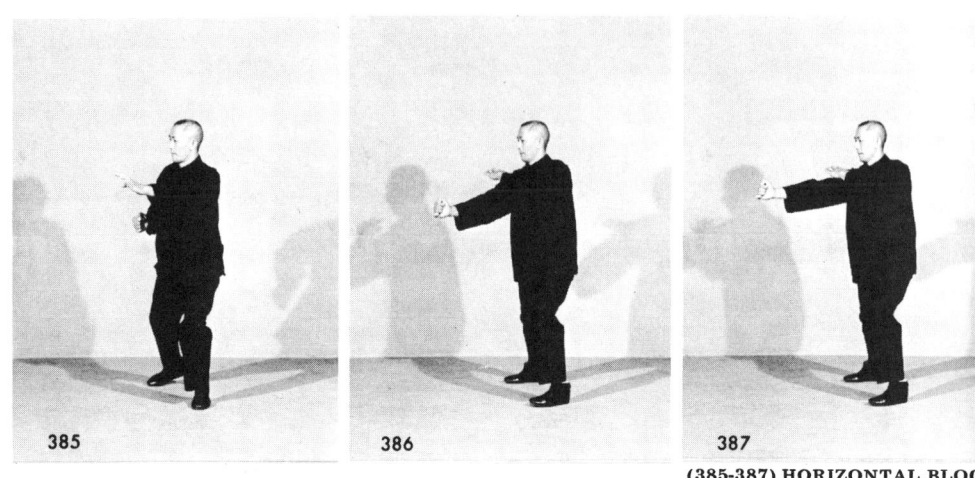

(385-387) HORIZONTAL BLOCK AND VERTICAL PUNCH

From the outstretched hand position, (385) slide your right foot back so you are faced toward the right, (386) simultaneously moving your left hand, palm down, toward your chest as you (387) deliver a right hand vertical punch.

(391) Pivot completely around on your left foot until (392) you are facing in the opposite direction. Simultaneously prepare for the slice block by raising both hands and (393) slicing the right hand over the left arm.

(388-390) TIGER CLAW

(388) As you move your right hand downward to protect your lower body, (389) move your left foot back into a gung bo stance, (390) simultaneously raising your left hand in a circular motion for the tiger claw technique.

(394) SLICE BLOCK

(394) Continue to extend both arms outward. (395) Swing both hands high to your left then (396) quickly downward in an arc, protecting your head with the right and executing an uppercut with your left.

(395-397) LEFT UPPERCUT

(397) After executing the left uppercut, prepare to execute a right uppercut by (398) swinging your arms high to the right. (399) Step off with your left foot as you begin to swing your arms in a downward arc.

(402-405) SLICE BLOCK

(403) The slice block is completed when both arms are fully outstretched. (404) Shift your body into a ma bo position and (405) return your right fist to your hip.

(398-401) RIGHT UPPERCUT

(400 & 401) Deliver the right uppercut punch and a left upper block as you move into a gung bo position. (402) Then in one, continuous motion execute a left slice block by slicing your left hand over your right arm.

(406) Begin a left eagle beak block by (407) rotating your left hand clockwise. (408) Your thumb should be tucked in, but your other fingers are extended.

(406-410) EAGLE BEAK BLOCK

(409 & 410) As you complete the left eagle beak block, (411) prepare to deliver a right corkscrew punch by moving into a gung bo stance.

(413-415) BACK FIST STRIKE   **(416-417) SLICE BLOCK**

(415) Deliver a left back fist punch as you shift into a gung bo position. (416) Then execute a right slice block, (417) continuing your movement until you are in a ma bo position with your hands outstretched.

(411-412) CORKSCREW PUNCH

(412) Deliver the right corkscrew punch. (413) Then twist your body to the right, (414) swinging the right arm in a semi-arc direction in preparation for a left back fist punch.

(418-419) EAGLE BEAK BLOCK

(418) Place your left fist on your hip and (419) execute a right eagle beak block by rotating your hands counterclockwise. (420) Prepare to deliver a left corkscrew punch.

(420-421) CORKSCREW PUNCH

(421) Deliver the left corkscrew punch. (422) Then face your left, using your left arm for blocking. (423) Step slightly forward with your left foot into a gung bo stance as you unleash a back fist strike.

(427) After delivery of the vertical punch, execute an uppercut strike by (428) swinging your right hand downward and (429) upward in a semi-circular motion. Your left hand protects your chest.

(422-424) BACK FIST STRIKE (425-426) VERTICAL PUNCH**

(424) Delivery of the back fist strike is made with a snapping motion of the hips. (425) Pull the left foot back into a ma bo stance (426) as you deliver a vertical punch, simultaneously sliding the right hand over the left.

(427-430) RIGHT UPPERCUT (431-432) LEFT ELBOW BLOCK**

(430) After delivery of the uppercut, (431) retract your right open hand, palm down, to your waist, with your left hand held vertically. (432) Then begin a left elbow block by twisting your body to the right.

(433-434) RIGHT ELBOW BLOCK

(433) Execute the right elbow block by retracting the left open hand to your waist. (434) Then, with your right hand held vertically, twist your body forcefully to the right. (435) Prepare to move into a lau ma stance.

(439) Continue to pivot to your left until (440) you have completed a 180-degree turn. (441) Shift into a gung bo stance, ready to deliver a right tiger claw.

(435-438) DOUBLE-HAND HORIZONTAL BLOCK

(436) Move into the lau ma stance by lifting your right foot and pivoting on your left. (437 & 438) At the same time, use both your open hands for blocking.

(439-443) TIGER CLAW

(442) Raise your right hand, leaving the left hand to protect the groin area. (443) Execute the right tiger claw, (444) then begin the closing form by moving your left foot back.

141

CLOSING THE FORM (444-449)

(445) With your feet together and hands outstretched to the sides, raise your arms to shoulder height, (446) bringing both hands together, (447) your left hand covering the right fist.

END

(448) Then lower both hands to their sides as (449) you complete the closing form.

Applications of Choy Lay Fut

The applied techniques in the following section are divided into defense and counter techniques and attacking techniques.

Defense and Counter Techniques

No martial arts system is complete unless those practicing it can translate the abstract (kata) into living reality (unrehearsed free sparring). To advance from the former to the latter requires years of practice. The succeeding pages are but the first step in a thousand-mile journey. The prerequisites of effective free fighting are endurance, power, timing, speed, and keen mental awareness. The techniques in this chapter must be practiced with these objectives in mind.

Since Choy Lay Fut is a fighting *system*, all aspects (kata and techniques) must be practiced as parts of the whole. The kata training will enhance the effectiveness of the attack and counter techniques in this chapter. The practice of the techniques will enhance the performance of the kata. The use of concentration and imagination is vital in the practice of all phases of Choy Lay Fut.

Back Fist Counter Against Grabbing Attack

(1) Stand in a ready position with both hands up and your left foot forward. (2) When your opponent reaches out to initiate a grab-and-punch attack, (3) quickly step forward with your right leg into a horse stance, simultaneously deflecting your opponent's grabbing arm downward with a scraping block. (4) Before he regains balance, (5) counter with a back fist strike to the bridge of your opponent's nose. All your countering movements must be executed simultaneously and explosively before your opponent can regain balance.

Vertical Punch Counter Against Wheel Kick

(1) Stand in a ready position with both hands up and your left foot forward. (2) When your opponent attacks with a right wheel kick, (3) cross block with your right hand and (4) simultaneously grip his leg with both hands. (5) As he moves forward, (6) use your right leg to sweep his supporting foot for the takedown, (7) then follow through immediately with (8) a vertical punch to the groin.

Tiger Claw Counter Against Front Kick

(1) Stand in a ready position with both hands up and your left foot forward. (2) As your opponent attempts a front snap kick, (3-4) step slightly to your left to avoid the attack, and hook block the kick with your left hand. (5) Lift his leg higher with your left arm as you step forward with your right foot, placing it behind his left foot. (6) Execute a tiger claw attack to your opponent's face and eyes as you (7) sweep his left foot and throw him backward.

Scraping Punch Counter

(1) Stand in a ready position with both hands up in a southpaw stance and your right foot forward. (2) When your opponent attempts a right front snap kick—right punch combination, (3) use an inside-hand, eagle beak block to deflect his kick, simultaneously turning your hip toward the kick while blocking. (4) Bring your left hand up quickly to block your opponent's right punch, (5) then quickly execute a scraping punch to his temple with the second knuckle of your fist. Deliver the strike in a swinging, scraping motion.

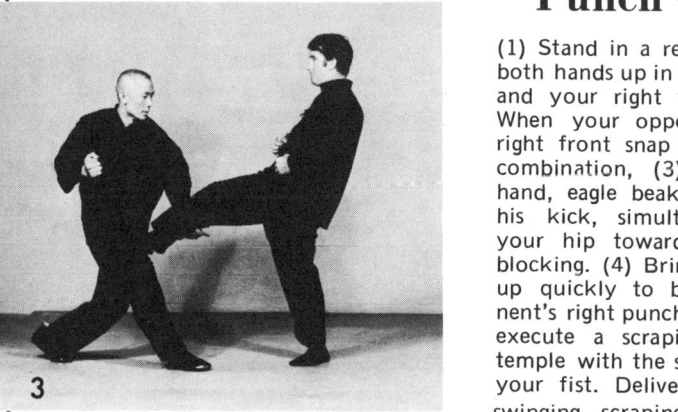

Right-Left Uppercut Counter

(1) Stand in a ready position. (2) When your opponent attempts a right lunge punch, (3) block and (4) counter with a right uppercut to the chest. (5) Then block his left hook with your right and counter with a left uppercut by stepping in with the right foot.

Back Fist Counter to Face

(1) Stand in a ready position. (2) When your opponent attacks with (3) a spinning back kick, (4) stop the kick with an eagle beak block. (5) As his leg descends, (6) step in quickly and (7) counter with a back fist strike to the bridge of his nose.

2

4

5

7

Vertical Punch Counter

(1) Stand in a ready position with both hands up and your left foot forward. (2) When your opponent lunges in to attempt a double leg takedown, (3) take a half-step with your rear foot and (4) raise your knee, (5) causing your opponent to lift his head back. (6 & 7) Simultaneously execute a vertical punch to his chin.

Corkscrew Punch with Finger Jab and Uppercut Counter

(1) Stand in a ready position. (2) When your opponent attempts a right front kick—left hook—right cross combination, (3) deflect his kick with a lower block and (4) simultaneously move in to (5) counter with a right corkscrew punch to his groin. (6) In the same motion block your opponent's left with a right circular block, and (7) counter with a left finger jab to his eye. (8) Then block with your left open hand and (9) step in quickly with a right uppercut to the chin.

Chop and Scissor Throw Counter

(1) Stand in a ready position. (2) When your opponent attempts a left jab, (3) block and trap his left arm, (4) then jerk it and step behind his left leg to execute a right chop to his throat. (5 & 6) Sweep your opponent's left leg with your right, (7) then spin around and (8) deliver a punch to his temple. Control your opponent's body during the counter by maintaining your grip on his right arm.

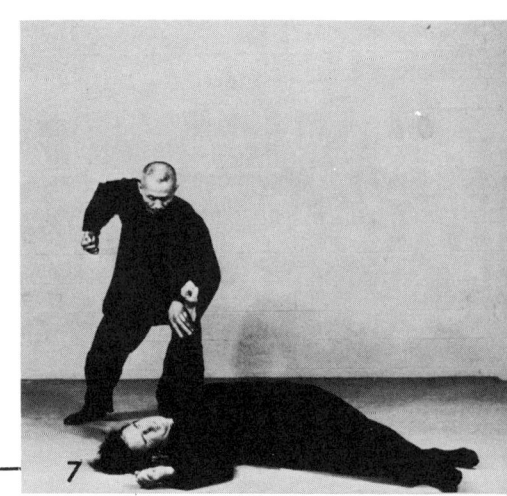

159

Slice Block with Vertical Punch Counter

(1) Stand in a ready position. (2) When your opponent attempts a right punch to your face, (3) block with your left hand and (4) counter to his body. When he blocks and seizes your right hand, (5) execute a left slice block by bringing your left open hand under his grabbing left hand. (6) Then slice and jerk back with your right fist in order to (7) punch to your off-balance opponent's head.

Finger Jab Counter to Throat

(1) Stand in a ready position. (2) When your opponent attacks with a right lunge punch, (3) use a left, open-hand block and (4) grab his right wrist. Then jerk him forward and (5) simultaneously execute a right finger jab to the Adam's apple. The grabbing, jerking and stepping in should be done quickly and smoothly before the attacker can recover or initiate a counterattack.

Finger Jab with Vertical Punch Counter

(1) Stand in a ready position. (2) When your opponent attempts a left-right combination technique, block with both open hands, (3) trapping his right arm with your left and countering with a left finger jab to the eye. (4) As your opponent executes a right punch, block with your left hand and step forward with your right foot, jerking his right arm slightly toward you. Then execute a right vertical punch to the chin.

Elbow Counter

(1) Stand in a ready position. (2) When your opponent attempts a right lunge punch, block with your left open hand and (3) trap his right arm as you simultaneously step in with your right foot and (4) deliver elbow strikes to his jaw and (5-7) sternum.

Back Fist, Vertical Punch and Uppercut Counter

(1) Stand in a ready position. (2) When your opponent attempts a right lunge punch—left uppercut—right hook combination, block his right punch and (3) counter with a (4) right back fist strike to the face. (5) Block his left uppercut with your right hand and (6) deliver a left vertical punch to his chin. (7) Then block his right hook, step in with your right foot and (8) deliver a right uppercut to the chin. Execute all punches in a quick, continuous motion.

Note: While it is true that the first blow may be all that is necessary in a combat situation, blocking and punching should be practiced in combinations as much as possible. Counter combinations such as this back fist—vertical punch—uppercut variety can deny an advantage to your opponent even when he is able to get off two and three-attack offensive combinations.

Elbow Blocks and Back Fist Counter

(1) If your opponent is in an orthodox stance, prepare to confront him by assuming an unorthodox, southpaw stance. (2) Block your opponent's left punch by turning your body toward the blow and blocking inward (to your left) with your right elbow. (3) When your opponent switches to a right punch, step back with your right foot, turn slightly toward the blow and block with your left elbow. (4) When your opponent reverts to a left punch, step back with your left foot and block with your right elbow. (5) When your opponent attempts a right punch, step back with your right foot and block with your left elbow. (6) When your opponent continues with still another left punch, pull back slightly, (7) block and (8) trap his left hand as you quickly execute a back fist strike to the temple. This sequence offers excellent practice in mental concentration in the face of an aggressive multiple attack.

Hook Throw-Punch Counter

(1) Stand in a ready position with both hands up and your left foot forward. (2) As your opponent attempts a skipping side kick, (3) trap his left leg

with a left circular block. (4) Then step in with your right foot and (5) sweep your opponent's supporting leg. (6) Follow through with a punch to the groin.

Elbow Counter Against Grab and Punch

The grab and punch is one of the most frequently used techniques in tournaments today. Properly execuled, it is a good point-getter. To counter the grab and punch, (1) stand in a ready position with both hands up and your left foot forward. (2) When your opponent attempts to grab your arm in preparation for a right hand punch, (3) grab his left arm as you (4) step slightly to your right. (5) Step in quickly with a right elbow smash to the temple. Timing is essential to the successful execution of the counter.

Attack Techniques

Most martial arts place heavy emphasis on defense and counter-offense. The importance placed on blocking techniques is a case in point. A great deal of time is devoted to techniques for countering specific attacks, as in karate's one-step sparring and the self-defense techniques of some systems. It is my opinion, however, that there is a time and place for initiating the attack. There are occasions for which "a good offense is the best defense," such as in tournaments where winning depends upon scoring points, and in a life-or-death encounter.

This section is designed to illustrate the basic Choy Lay Fut techniques that can be used offensively. In each case, effective feinting and bridging the gap quickly are prerequisites to successfully executing an attack.

Arm Grab, Vertical Punch, Foot Sweep and Vertical Punch Combination

(1) Stand in a ready position with both hands up and your left foot forward. (2) Without telegraphing your movement, (3) quickly grab your opponent's hand. (4) Step in with your right foot to deliver a right vertical punch to his temple, (5) and in a continuous motion, sweep his left foot. (6) Then turn and kneel down, (7) still holding his hand, (8) to deliver another punch to his head.

Lunging Vertical Punch Attack and Takedown

(1) Stand in a ready position. Look your opponent straight in the eyes, being sure not to telegraph your intentions. (2) Abruptly slap your opponent's left hand with your lead hand and (3) step in quickly with

your right foot, (4) placing it behind your opponent's left foot. (5) Execute a right fist punch to his face and (6) sweep his front foot with your right foot.

Combination Attack Hammer-Back Fist

(1) Stand in a ready position with both hands up and your left foot forward. (2) Slap your opponent's lead hand as you (3-4) step in with your right foot and place it at the inside of your opponent's left foot to prevent his retreat. (5) Retract your left hand as you execute a vertical punch to your opponent's face. (6-7) Then drop your hand down quickly and (8-9) deliver a circular back fist strike to the temple. Note: Your left hand remains in a protective ready position throughout these attacks. The combination must be executed quickly, smoothly and with continuity.

Arm Grab and Elbow Break with Back Fist Strike

(1) Stand in a ready position with both hands up and your left foot forward. (2) Seize your opponent's left wrist and (3) jerk him forward,

(4) simultaneously stepping forward with your right foot and placing it behind your opponent's left foot. Slam your right elbow into his left elbow. (5-6) Complete the combination with a back fist strike to your opponent's face.

Double Fake with Left Vertical Punch Attack

(1) Stand in a ready position with both hands up and your left foot forward. (2) Place your left foot forward and fake a left lead to your opponent's body. (3) When he blocks your left, (4) fake a right to his head. (5) When he counters with a left upper block, (6) hook his blocking hand with your right hand and (7) jerk it toward you as you execute a left vertical punch to his chin.

Fake Sweep, Back Fist Strike and Elbow Attack

(1) Stand in a ready position with both hands up and your left foot forward. (2) Fake a foot sweep by (3) lightly tapping your opponent's left leg with your right foot. (4) Then step in with your right foot behind his left leg, (5) grab his left wrist and (6) execute a back fist strike to the temple. After delivery of the back fist strike, (7) maintain your grip on his left wrist and (8) follow through with a right elbow strike to the face.

Feint Low Side Kick with Spinning Elbow Strike

(1) Stand in a ready position with both hands up and your left foot forward. (2 & 3) Push your oppo-

nent's lead leg lightly with your left foot, then (4) pivot clockwise and (5) execute a right elbow attack (6) to the face. Be sure to snap your head toward your right shoulder as you pivot. All movements must be done quickly and abruptly.

Feint Kick with Back Fist Strike

(1) Stand in a ready position with both hands up and your left foot forward. (2) Feint a right front kick. (3) As your defender attempts to block it, (4) quickly pivot on your right foot and (5) execute a circular block with your left hand (6) to trap his left arm. (7) Deliver a right back fist strike to his face. Note: The feint front kick should be made quickly, but lightly enough so that you don't over-commit yourself or lose your balance.

Feint Low Hook Kick to High Hook Kick Attack

(1) Stand in a ready position with both hands up and your left foot forward. (2) Feint a left kick to your opponent's groin or knee. (3) As he lowers his guard to block the kick, (4) deliver a roundhouse kick to his face.

Fake Low Hook Kick with a Left Vertical Punch-Back Fist Strike

(1) Stand in a ready position with both hands up and your left foot forward. (2) Feint a left hook kick to your opponent's groin, (3) then, as he reacts, (4) execute a left vertical punch to his face. (5) Quickly trap his left hand with your left and immediately execute a circular back fist strike to the temple.